Moon Landing Day

poems by

Alissa Sammarco

Finishing Line Press
Georgetown, Kentucky

Moon Landing Day

Copyright © 2024 by Alissa Sammarco
ISBN 979-8-88838-587-6 First Edition
All rights reserved under International and Pan-American Copyright Conventions. No part of this book may be reproduced in any manner whatsoever without written permission from the publisher, except in the case of brief Quotations embodied in critical articles and reviews.

ACKNOWLEDGMENTS

Moon Landing Day and The Power of the Dog first appeared in *Black Moon Magazine*
The Look of You first appeared in *Sheila-Na-Gig Online*
To Sleep first appeared in *Change Seven*
Maybe I Promised You I'd Be Better first appeared in the 2021 LexPoMo Anthology, *But There Was Fire in the Distance*

Publisher: Leah Huete de Maines
Editor: Christen Kincaid
Cover Art: Susan Crew
Author Photo: Troi Gray
Cover Design: Elizabeth Maines McCleavy

Order online: www.finishinglinepress.com
also available on amazon.com

Author inquiries and mail orders:
Finishing Line Press
PO Box 1626
Georgetown, Kentucky 40324
USA

Contents

Acknowledgment 1

Dearest 2

Maybe I Promised I'd Be Better 3

This Is the Name It Shall Be Called, the LORD
    Our Righteousness 4

Confessions 5

Why So Many Bullets 6

Sour Oranges 7

The Power of the Dog 8

I am the Thin Blue Line 9

Moon Landing Day 10

To Sleep 11

Stone Soup 12

Who Raised the Children? 13

The Look of You 14

I Wanted to Call You from LaGuardia 15

Not Even Once More 16

Regrets 18

The Last Blue Sky 18

This book is dedicated to my dear ones who have won and my dear ones who have lost battles with addiction and abuse. Some of these poems were inspired by a call from an old friend who apologized to me. I hung up the phone and realized that the call was the Ninth Step of the Twelve Step Program. These patterns are passed from one generation to the next and are so often unheard and unseen. For all who survive, I see you.

Acknowledgment

It was not the wine
that made me sick.
Waves of heavy lumbering draught
curled over the deck,
and the dark plain
cast its shadow over my soul.

We trimmed our sails
against the wind of our enemies
before the battle began.

On the bluffs, our daughters watched
blowing kisses to those who perished,
their gossamer skirts plastered to pale legs.

I was true, once,
before the battle,
before my love knew what I was.

Oh wind, be silent
or let my love be deaf.
It would kill him
to hear the Kraken's call
as it breached the plane.

Oh blind seas, take me down deep
before the black waves
give way to rainbow spray
in tomorrow's sunrise.

Save me that.

Dearest,

I am writing to keep us safe,
to tuck us away in a place where we will not spoil.
It was only an offhanded comment, but it sent me running.

It was all I could do to hold myself together.
You, seemingly adoring, finding only what is wrong.
All those little things I cannot keep track of,
leaving a light on, the shades open, a dish in the sink,
sit between us.

But you I never forget.
You live in the back of my mind.
sharing meals, pouring coffee,
kissing goodnight.

So now, we've come to this place
where words are dismissive,
where eyes are cold,
and my heart tucked away for safety.

I thought we had learned our lesson
of how to behave, drunk or sober.
And yet we still walk old paths in old shoes,
treads bare, sliding downhill.
Let us grip each other and find our footing again.

For what has happened that cannot be mended?

Love A.

Maybe I Promised I'd Be Better

Maybe I promised you something I couldn't deliver,
as I drove over the roads I knew so well, all the way to the river.

Maple leaves and Indian cigars hung over the road
like a bad haircut, bangs sticking in my eyes.

I couldn't see the sky and swerved too fast through curves
until the Kellogg on—ramp where we parked boats at marinas

and bottles of bourbon at Annie's joint.
Maybe I promised you I'd be better

than a coffee cup filled with booze and fake tattoos
at two a.m., last call closing down the place,

waiting for someone to walk me to my car,
waiting for someone to drive me home.

Take my keys,
take me.

This Is the Name It Shall Be Called, the LORD Our Righteousness

(Jeremiah 33:16)

Jerusalem,
      city where David reigned,
      will you save me from addiction?

Fingers playing harps strung tight across the city gate.
To pass through I must separate limbs from body,
slide between strings, careful not to strike a chord,
abdicate my thorny crown and admit I am powerless.

Confessions
        sound like tears sliding down veined cheeks,
        capillaries burst by holy water and wine.

Forgiveness
        comes like black cassocks
        that sway in windy prayer.

Did I follow cloven hooves only to end up here,
where angels wield sword and shepherd's crook?
Your city grows fat and breeds deer
without fear of wolves.

Salt and cracked corn left out to draw them in.
Oh, how I coveted their fearlessness,
and at 16, drove my car 100 miles an hour
just as the doe stepped into the street.

And the priests, they bowed their heads,
sipped wine, broke bread,
and called the city by its name.

Confessions

The hard and soft sound
from tongue to lips forming
the ministry of worship,
secular sentiment steeped
in the sweet breath
of dreams and dreamers.

At night, I surrender to touch,
begging to be scratched,
and confess faults
behind a curtain of champagne.

The chit-chit of fear
facing the sudden ouster
from this sublime embrace
of this place where everything is fuzzy.

Will anything remain
for my children to divvy up?
Or will I take all my treasures with me?

These are my confessions.
They tumble like river rocks
until smooth and round,
lying just below the water
that, like the veil of the confessional,
masks the true shape and size of them.

Why So Many Bullets

Maiming children in their sleep?
Parents point derringer fingers
across the living room.

Why so many missed chances
built on church ruins that crumble
in sympathetic resonance to gospel choirs.

Lovers shoot heartbeats like gunfire
through cell phones.

Stray bullets find their way
from the next block,
silence that pop-pop.

Sour Oranges

The Seville oranges have arrived.
Their firm dimpled skin, round in my palm,
smells like youth as I breath in promises,
small oily beads under fingernails,
peeling back the rind.
I pull it in half, then sections, anticipating.

> *Why did you lie to me,*
> *to my every sense, mouth watering,*
> *eyes glowering, heart aching.*

Lips part and teeth pierce flesh,
shocked by bitterness.

> *And in that moment,*
> *all the world lost its sweetness.*

The Power of the Dog

> *Deliver Me from the Sword, My Soul from the Power of the Dog.*
> *Psalms 22:20*

Ice cubes clink
under paper umbrellas
while the ocean swallows my regrets
popping them into her mouth
one after another like bar nuts.

The dog barks in his low fast phrases,
warding off strangers.
Trained to sniff out sickness,
he tracks that sour mead in the morning,
a cancer crowding my brain.

I know the smell of him too,
wet and full of earth,
the taste of salt on my lips.
I have no breathy sighs in the end.
I cry out, forsaken.

Oh God, have you left me
at the mercy of my enemies?
While the dog sits on his haunches,
teeth bared, licking his lips,
and filling his belly with his own vomit.

I am the Thin Blue Line

Shooting off into space, I push higher
through an atmosphere that burns my face
while g-forces hold my eyelids so I can not blink.

I burst through sound barriers
with sonic booms that turns heads.

Chemtrails map a course between oceans
of liquor, their ice cube islands floating
between conversations, clinking against teeth
and fingers fishing with barbed hooks.

I skim these waves,
bounce off the swell
back into the atmosphere.

As I reach an apex, the rockets explode,
crashing into the sea.
My separation complete.

And me, a head full of stardust and moonshine,
full of rocket fuel cocktails,
I stretch out into a single, tightly drawn line
as I orbit the earth.

Moon Landing Day

Tides move back and forth
seven miles above the Mariana Trench

where fish with luminescent spines
and giant red worms sip sulfur from volcanic vents.

The moon, gray and white,
circles like a ball on a string.

Man cannot breathe in space,
nor under a thousand tons of water.

And on that day when man stood on the moon,
breathing in weightless vanity,

all of air and water and weird creatures
rose to the surface and exploded.

To Sleep

Did you cry yourself to sleep
when the rain was a comet
making rivers through the back yard
that lit up like ice
trailing celestial missiles?

Did you moan and shriek
until your eyes popped from their sockets,
throat swollen tight?
No hot lemonade and rum burns quite like that.

And the rain tastes like
red match tips held between your teeth
just before they ignite
in powder blue flames.

If only for a moment,
silence would smother you
like kisses—
        they were not kisses.

Stone Soup

Seasoned with the tears
of friends and lovers. We salivated
like dogs at the butcher's back door,
stirring the pot with big wooden spoons,
complicit.

> *I reach in,*
> *pull out stones,*
> *one by one.*

My skin blistered and peeled
as I tried to make amends.

> *I make my list.*
> *I check off names.*
> *I feign deliverance.*

The soup simmered,
filling our house,
and we savored it together.
So how was this now my responsibility?

> *I make my list,*
> *but I will not share this with you.*

Who Raised the Children?

Who raised the children?
Voices speaking in moral certitudes,
staying the hand if not the tongue
when hard lessons must be learned.

Who said you must have
a his and hers, a forever after?
Does that make all the things said acceptable
while neighbors listen from their patio?

Does it make it any better
that a woman and a man
teach their children
with the words they swallow,
the words they spit out?

These lessons are as ancient as angels and gods.

The Look of You

You look like your brother.
You always resented him,
the first born, the favorite,
and you, like a bastard,
beaten with an antique billy club
before the police came and confiscated it.
They left you behind
in a palace with winding paths
through gardens your mother planted.
She grew flowers and hasta
in shadows underneath the trees
and in bright exposed beds.
You picked her tulips,
she cracked your knuckles with a wooden spoon
but put them in a vase, nonetheless.
Maybe you really did love once.
Maybe you didn't.
But when you turned those lessons on me,
you never averted your eyes,
sleepwalking, deaf to my pleas,
blind to the handfuls of hair and wretchedness
that remained.
What you really broke was your own heart,
empty after the flash flood of familial suffering,
pretending you had ever let me in.

I Wanted to Call You from LaGuardia

My plane landed early at LaGuardia,
and I thought of that time when you and your father
picked me up, driving through the city and over the bridge.
You told me later that "people just don't drive there."

Your father explained about the Port Authority,
and trains in Grand Central Station.
I wanted to hold your hand,
in the backseat of his Buick.

As I watched the men on the tarmac,
I wanted to call you just to let you know
that I can take a bus, a subway,
that I've seen the clock at Grand Central Station,

that you feel so close I can almost touch you,
yet as far away as our fingertips
in the back seat of your father's sedan.

Not Even Once More

What if it just ended
and I never wrote another poem,
not another line.
What if the storm stopped blowing
and the waters became stagnant,
smelling of our last meal
turned to muck
stinking when the eddies stop spinning.
What if you turned away
and never kissed me,
not even once more,
and our currents became still,
smelling of sour milk and sweat,
like the bed where we slept,
leaving the swell and pitch of it
behind.

Regrets

I thought I'd gathered them all up,
one by one, and put them in my pocket.
I was wrong to think that I could.

There's always one or two
that slip through your fingers,
falling to the ground to be left behind.

A pocket full is not enough
when the Devil taunts you, thumbing his nose,
waiving his tail from across the street.

It's like following the breadcrumbs
that Hansel and Gretel dropped
on their way to see the witch.

The deeper into the forest you go
the fewer the breadcrumbs
the more desperate you are to find them.

You know where the witch lives
and what she will do when you find her.
But you have no choice except to keep going

down that dark path following them,
collecting each breadcrumb in your pocket,
even though you'll never find your way home.

The Last Blue Sky

Fades in shades of blue & pink & gray.
The leaves have fallen and
I can see Jupiter and Saturn,
Scorpio striking stings at their heels.
This second summer leaves
as quietly as he stepped in,
turning away his blue eyed gaze
from our steep slide back to earth.
A thin blue line snapped by the weight
of Pisces' thrashing in shallow waters
as they leap great waterfalls
to where they end & begin again.

Alissa Sammarco lives, writes and practices law in Cincinnati, Ohio. The razor-sharp imagery and sometimes musical incantations speak plainly to our everyday life, with turns that surprise in each poem. Her poetry has appeared in print and online journals including *Sheila-Na-Gig, Black Moon Magazine, Change Seven, Quiet Diamonds, Main Street Rag, Evening Street Review, Stone Canoe, But There Was Fire in the Distance, Yearling, VIA: Voices of Italian Americana, Hags on Fire, the 2021* and *2022 Lexington Poetry Month Anthologies*. She has authored two chapbooks, *Beyond the Dawn*, and *I See Them Now*.

Find more information and poetry at *www.AlissaSammarco.com* and Instagram @AlissaSammarcoWrites.

www.ingramcontent.com/pod-product-compliance
Lightning Source LLC
Chambersburg PA
CBHW070654100426
42734CB00048B/2992